THE LOVE STORY OF TWO AMAZING BALD EAGLES

Second Edition

ANN PARRIS-STEWART

Copyright © 2024 Ann Parris-Stewart.

Originally published as "The Love Story of Two Bald Eagles"
Copyright © 2017 by Ann Parris-Stewart

All rights reserved. No part of this book may be reproduced, stored, or transmitted by any means—whether auditory, graphic, mechanical, or electronic—without written permission of both publisher and author, except in the case of brief excerpts used in critical articles and reviews. Unauthorized reproduction of any part of this work is illegal and is punishable by law.

ISBN: 979-8-89419-446-2 (sc)
ISBN: 979-8-89419-447-9 (hc)
ISBN: 979-8-89419-448-6 (e)

Because of the dynamic nature of the Internet, any web addresses or links contained in this book may have changed since publication and may no longer be valid. The views expressed in this work are solely those of the author and do not necessarily reflect the views of the publisher, and the publisher hereby disclaims any responsibility for them.

One Galleria Blvd., Suite 1900, Metairie, LA 70001
1-888-421-2397

To my daughter, Nedra Stewart; my son, Alwyn Stewart; my daughter-in-law, Lakiah Stewart; my grandsons, Nile Jean and Aiden Stewart; my sister, Merlene Parris; and my brother, Canute Parris, who all consistently supported, encouraged, and cheered me on throughout this endeavor.

ACKNOWLEDGMENTS

Thanks to my editor, Maxine A. Wiggan, the first professional writer and copy editor who reviewed the manuscript for this book, determined that this story was worth publishing, and assisted with its editing.

Thanks to my wonderful children, Nedra and Alwyn. I love you both, always and forever, no matter what. I am proud of each of your accomplishments.

Thanks to my daughter-in-law Lakiah for her love, care, and encouragement.

Thanks to my grandson Nile Jean, who was nine years old at the time this book was first published. His love for birds, especially the bald eagle, not only prompted me to write this story but also inspired his design of the cover page of this book.

Thanks to my grandson Aiden, who, although a baby, laughs whenever he sees a picture of the bald eagle.

Thanks to my sister Merlene and my brother Canute who always hear my heart and allow me to express my thoughts and feelings.

I am eternally grateful for all of you.

KEA AND SEMAJ

Kea and Semaj are two bald eagles who live in the southern area of Alaska.

"Come and perch beside me on this tall tree and let us view the beauty that surrounds this mountainous area of Alaska," said Kea, a beautiful bald eagle, to Semaj, her childhood male friend.

"Kea! This view is absolutely beautiful! I love it!" Semaj exclaimed.

"Did you know that bald eagles live only in the United States of America, USA for short?" continued Kea proudly.

"Oh, yes! And I hope you have noticed how similar we both are," added Semaj.

"Oh, yes! Oh, yes! As adults, we both have blackish-brown backs and chests, white heads, necks, and tails," said Kea confidently.

"Yellow feet, legs, and beaks," added Semaj.

"And pale-yellow eyes," they both said in unison as they began laughing.

"And don't forget," said Semaj, "we bald eagles have a life span of thirty years."

"Yep!" agreed Kea.

THE AMERICAN EMBLEM

A soft wind gently swayed the branch on which the eagles were sitting. As the warm sunlight seeped through the upper branches, Semaj reflectively added, "My great-grandfather told me that in 1782, the Founding Fathers chose the bald eagle as the national bird of the United States of America."

"And you know what, Semaj," chimed in Kea, "I am so proud to know that we, bald eagles, are the national bird and emblem of the greatest country in the world, the United States of America."

"Kea," added Semaj, "I think we were chosen because we symbolize pride, independence, courage, and strength."

"I totally agree with you, Semaj. We are also protected under the National Emblem Act of 1940 and the Endangered Species Act of 1972."

"My, my, my, aren't we special!" Semaj proudly proclaimed.

Kea smiled. "Yes, indeed," she said, as they both reflected on the first day they met.

THE COURTSHIP

Semaj and Kea met at a birthday party when they were children and became close friends, visiting each other daily. Now, as they continued relaxing in each other's company, Semaj warmly expressed, "Oh, Kea, you are such a good friend and companion. You have stolen my heart. I love you so much. Can we be mates for life?"

Kea's eyes became soft and glowed in the sunlight as she tenderly whispered, "I would love that so very much, Semaj." The two eagles snuggled closer together, basking in the sunshine, and were very quiet for a few moments. Then Kea softly suggested, "Semaj, if we are going to be mates for life, we should start our pair-bonding."

"Our what?" teased Semaj, then quickly added, "I agree. We should begin courting each other. Do you realize this is very similar to being married?"

"Yep," said Kea very softly, as they both gazed into each other's eyes.

As the days passed, Semaj and Kea continued courting. They chased each other through the air, zigzagging, diving, and soaring high over the mountainous landscapes. Sometimes they locked their talons together and cartwheeled downward. After breaking loose, they again soared over tremendous heights, alternately yelling to each other, "Catch me if you can!"

One afternoon, just before they broke loose from soaring, Kea whispered, "Semaj, our courtship is great fun, and I am so very happy being with you."

"Yes," agreed Semaj, "it is fun to be in love with you, and I, too, am extremely happy to have you in my life, especially for the last three months that we have been courting."

MAKING THE NEST

A few days later, as the couple sat on a branch watching the sunset, Kea smilingly whispered, as they embraced, "We have been courting for a very long time. I think it is time for us to start a family."

"Yes, yes, my beloved. It is time," whispered Semaj. "We will build a nest so that our children will have a comfortable home in which to live and play."

"Let's find the tallest tree overlooking the ocean," said Kea excitedly.

"That's a great idea! And we will have easy access to various types of fishes and sea creatures to feed ourselves and nourish our children. You are so very smart, sweet wife."

Both eagles smiled and snuggled closer together.

The next day, Semaj and Kea found a tall tree near a lake. There they built a nest on the very top. First, they used large sticks to build the foundation of the nest, and then they lined it with twigs, thorns, dried leaves, grass, and soft materials such as feathers. They knew the nest had to be enormous because they are very large birds.

THE EGGS

After several days, the large, sturdy nest was completed. Kea laid two smooth, off-white eggs.

"My beloved Kea," whispered Semaj, "we have to take turns sitting on the eggs to keep them warm so that they will hatch."

"I know. This is our incubation period, and the brood patches on our chests will help to keep our eggs nice and warm." Kea smiled.

"Yep, and this is so because our brood patches have few feathers but many blood vessels," replied Semaj.

"Yes, and these brood patches come into close contact with our eggs when we sit on them," added Kea.

"Okay, then," replied Semaj with great excitement, "we have about thirtyfive days to go, so let the fun begin!"

ARDEN AND ELIN ARRIVE

For the next thirty-five days, the couple alternated hunting for food so that one bird would be sitting on the eggs at all times. They had lots of fun together, lovingly sharing jokes, laughing, singing, and planning for their babies while snuggling close together every chance they got. They graciously and patiently awaited the arrival of the new members of their family.

On the thirty-sixth day of the incubation period, Kea excitedly said to Semaj, "I hear a pecking sound coming from the inside of one of the eggs. What do you think that could be?"

"My beloved Kea, I think one of our babies is ready to be hatched."

"Oh, yes," said Kea, "the baby is using the hard bump on its beak to push against the inside of the egg."

"That hard bump is called an egg tooth," added Semaj with a glitter in his eyes, "and our baby will keep pushing against the egg until it cracks."

The pecking sound continued. After thirty-six hours, the first baby eagle emerged, appearing exhausted.

"Welcome to the world, precious child! The soft white down that your body is covered with is so very beautiful," said Kea softly.

"You are a girl, and your name is Arden," whispered Semaj.

A day later, the other egg hatched. "You, adorable child, welcome!" Kea smiled.

"You are a boy, and your name is Elin," whispered Semaj.

Then he continued, "Children, your mother and I know that you are both very tired from the tedious task of hatching. Just rest."

"We will keep you warm, feed you, remove the broken eggshells from the nest, and watch over you," Kea lovingly added. Both Arden and Elin were happy to hear that because they were tired and sleepy.

HOW FAST THEY GROW

A week after the eaglets were born, Semaj exclaimed to Kea, "Look! Our children are growing beautifully! The soft white down that they were born with has been replaced with a coarse gray down."

"Yes," Kea replied, "and their egg teeth have fallen out."

As their growth progressed, the eaglets learned how to take food from their parents' beaks. Both parents watched with pride as the children instinctively hopped around the nest and flapped their wings.

"Good job, children!" exclaimed Kea. "Flapping your wings will make them strong and will prepare you for flying."

Semaj chimed in, "You have mastered these skills quickly. We are so proud of you."

"We will continue to feed you until you are old enough to hunt food for yourselves," explained Kea.

"While we continue to feed you, beak to beak, you can also begin to feed yourselves with the scraps of meat that drop into the nest," Semaj encouraged.

"Yes, father," replied Elin and Arden in unison.

After a few more weeks, the eaglets' bodies gradually changed from the gray down stage to the feathering stage. Feathers began to grow on their backs, chests, shoulders, and wings.

Their father, Semaj, said to them, "Children, you can actually start hopping around from branch to branch."

"Oh really, Dad?" Arden and Elin asked as they excitedly hopped out of the nest, flapping their wings, as they landed on nearby branches. "This is so much fun!" They laughed.

"We were so looking forward to hopping on these branches," said Elin with a look of glee in his eyes.

TIME TO FLY

After a couple of weeks, it was time to learn to fly. Semaj and Kea explained the process to Arden and Elin. By this time, the eaglets had become very good at hopping from branch to branch and were having lots of fun. They were now super excited about learning to fly.

In preparation for flying lessons, Semaj and Kea started removing the feathers and soft materials from inside the nest, tossing them over the edge of the nest unto the ground. Next, they removed the twigs and leaves. By this time, Arden and Elin were worried! Their nest was now almost only thorns, and it was no longer comfortable and cozy. They had to remain on the edge of the nest or on the nearby branches.

One day, Kea lovingly looked at Arden and Elin and softly whispered, "It's time!" Then she used her beak to gently push Elin off the branch he had just hopped onto. He started falling toward the ground. It was a long way down!

"Flap those wings!" yelled his dad. He was carefully watching Elin, ready to act if necessary.

"Flap those wings!" Kea shouted.

Elin was not doing such a good job, so Semaj speedily swooped down, swiftly passed Elin, and then glided smoothly under him, catching him on his back.

"Wow! That was super scary and super cool at the same time," exclaimed Elin.

"I am sure it was!" his dad replied. "We will keep trying this until you get excellent at it." He then gracefully flew back to the nest with Elin.

"Now it's your turn, Arden," said Kea as her eyes smiled at her beautiful and scared eaglet. "You can do this!" She gently nudged her off the branch. Down, down, down she went. "Flap your wings!" yelled Kea.

Arden flapped her wings a couple of times then stopped. Both parents kept their eyes on her. "Time for the rescue!" announced Semaj as he again swooped down, this time, to catch his precious baby girl. The family continued this exercise over and over until both Arden and Elin were soaring like eagles. They were having so much fun!

LEARNING TO HUNT

The beaks and talons of Arden and Elin grew quickly. Their bodies also got larger. They were now skilled at flying and strong enough to hunt for food. Their parents, Semaj and Kea, taught them how to use their beaks for tearing food and their talons for hunting.

The eaglets learned how to hunt for reptiles, such as turtles and snakes. They hunted for small mammals such as rabbits. Waterfowls, such as flamingoes, and smaller birds were also on their menu. They were not even afraid of catching antelopes and sheep. They also feasted on some dead animals. Swooping down into the ocean and grabbing fishes were also things these eaglets were taught to do.

With lots of practice, they mastered these skills at the age of three months old and were experts at hunting. Semaj and Kea were so very proud of them. They knew that their eaglets were now fully prepared to become independent. They were not too sure though, as parents, how they would handle their children leaving home to live on their own.

READY TO TAKE ON THE WORLD

At four months old, Arden and Elin expressed to their parents that they desired to be independent.

"Thank you, Mom and Dad, for loving us and caring for us. At this time, we feel that we can be on our own."

Parents and children embraced one another tearfully. "We love you, Mom and Dad. We will visit on our birthdays, on Thanksgiving, and at Christmas." They embraced for a long time and then said goodbye.

Arden and Elin flew away to find mates and had plans to start new lives with their own families. Tearfully embracing each other, Semaj and Kea watched

Arden and Elin fly away into the distance. After several minutes that seemed like forever, they looked into each other's eyes as Kea spoke without words. In response, Semaj whispered, "Yes, my darling, we can certainly have more babies." He spread his wings and embraced her.

THE END!

GLOSSARY

Mate — To come together to make eggs or babies

Pair — bonding — Eagles selecting a mate

Talons — The claws of birds of prey

Incubation — Keeping eggs warm so they will hatch

Brood patch — Bare area of skin on the chest of adult birds, used to keep the eggs warm

ABOUT THE AUTHOR

Ann Parris-Stewart is the mother of Nedra Ann Stewart and Alwyn James Stewart. She is also the grandmother of Nile Necker Jean and Aiden James Stewart and is a retired registered nurse residing in Kissimmee, Florida, USA. She holds a bachelor of science degree in health science and a master of science degree in gerontological nursing and was involved in several aspects of the nursing profession. For several years, Ann worked at the Veteran Administration Hospital, Bronx, New York, in various managerial capacities. She also worked in the capacity of director of nursing and administrator with a home health agency in Florida.

Ann has always been intrigued with birds and is especially fascinated with the bald eagle as the national emblem of the USA. Inspired by her grandson Nile, she wrote this book, incorporating several facts about the bald eagle into a beautiful love story.

www.ingramcontent.com/pod-product-compliance
Lightning Source LLC
LaVergne TN
LVHW070443070526
838199LV00036B/687